Lessons
the Afterlife

"This remarkable and wise book offers you, the reader, a deepened awareness of the truth of your Divine nature, of God or All Consciousness, and greater clarity about why you are here as a spiritual being in physical form. Imagine what Earth would be like if each human being embraced and lived out these basic truths. This book is a must-read for anyone on the path of spiritual growth and deepened inner knowing. But be forewarned: this book will awaken you, expand your consciousness, and offer you greater clarity about who you are and your purpose here."

JOHN P. FORSYTH, PH.D., PROFESSOR OF PSYCHOLOGY AND DIRECTOR OF THE ANXIETY DISORDERS RESEARCH PROGRAM AT SUNY ALBANY AND COAUTHOR OF *THE ANXIETY HAPPENS GUIDED JOURNAL*

"This extraordinary book, channeled by Jordan through his father, Matthew McKay, is a tour-de-force, seamlessly weaving cosmology, theology, quantum mechanics, transpersonal psychology, mysticism, and astrophysics into an engaging form. Jordan effortlessly dismantles the heretofore concrete barrier separating us from 'the other side' and gives us instead what we in Ireland call 'a thin place' that transforms the mundane into the mystical and the secular into the sacred. It is a rare gem of a book."

SEÁN ÓLAOIRE, AUTHOR OF *SETTING GOD FREE*

"*Lessons from the Afterlife* offers a profound path to finding spiritual answers from within. This book provides readers with suggestions about consciousness and the universe to consider and meditate on. Not only do you discover answers within but you also gain the ability to seek answers at any time once you know how to practice Deep Knowledge Meditation."

CATHARINE MEYERS, PUBLISHER AT
NEW HARBINGER PUBLICATIONS

"Many authors write about the afterlife, but McKay's channelings and locutions have a unique quality: they make the universe larger and more dimensional than it was a moment before. This is because he transmits the key distinction between ego self and soul that even many spiritual systems override."

RICHARD GROSSINGER, AUTHOR OF
BOTTOMING OUT THE UNIVERSE

"Matthew McKay's book invites the reader to contemplate the finite microcosm of personal existence by engaging in a dialogue with the infinite macrocosm of the universe. Bold, rich, and deeply thought-provoking, it is a true gem by a unique father and son who demonstrate the power of All."

AUSTYN WELLS, SPIRITUAL MEDIUM AND
AUTHOR OF SOUL CONVERSATIONS

"McKay takes a deep dive into examining the nature of reality, the meaning of life, and how to cope with loss. *Lessons from the Afterlife* reads like a personal guidebook to the essence of our existence."

JEFFREY C. WOOD, PSYD.,
COAUTHOR OF THE NEW HAPPINESS

"*Lessons from the Afterlife* is a rare find, as it offers a summary of the universe and our place in it that everyone can understand. These words will inspire you and offer profound wisdom."

PETER SMITH, AUTHOR OF QUANTUM CONSCIOUSNESS

Lessons from the Afterlife

A DEEP KNOWLEDGE
MEDITATION GUIDEBOOK

A Sacred Planet Book

Matthew McKay, Ph.D.

Park Street Press

Rochester, Vermont

Park Street Press
One Park Street
Rochester, Vermont 05767
www.ParkStPress.com

Text stock is SFI certified

Park Street Press is a division of Inner Traditions International

Sacred Planet Books are curated by Richard Grossinger, Inner Traditions editorial board member and cofounder and former publisher of North Atlantic Books. The Sacred Planet collection, published under the umbrella of the Inner Traditions family of imprints, includes works on the themes of consciousness, cosmology, alternative medicine, dreams, climate, permaculture, alchemy, shamanic studies, oracles, astrology, crystals, hyperobjects, locutions, and subtle bodies.

Cataloging-in-Publication Data for this title is available from the Library of Congress

ISBN 978-1-64411-940-2 (print)
ISBN 978-1-64411-941-9 (ebook)

Printed and bound in the United States by Lake Book Manufacturing, LLC
The text stock is SFI certified. The Sustainable Forestry Initiative® program promotes sustainable forest management.

10 9 8 7 6 5 4 3 2 1

Text design and layout by Virginia Scott Bowman
This book was typeset in Hypatia Sans and Legacy Sans with Caslon used as the display typeface

To send correspondence to the author of this book, mail a first-class letter to the author c/o Inner Traditions • Bear & Company, One Park Street, Rochester, VT 05767, and we will forward the communication, or contact the author directly at **matt@newharbinger.com**.

Scan the QR code and save 25% at InnerTraditions.com. Browse over 2,000 titles on spirituality, the occult, ancient mysteries, new science, holistic health, and natural medicine.

For my wife, Jude, with all my love

Contents

INTRODUCTION

Why Are We Here? What Is This Place?

HUMAN LIFE IS SURROUNDED with mystery. At the center of this mystery is the question: Why are we here? To break it down further: Why are we born, live brief lives full of uncertainty and struggle, and die on a small planet in a remote corner of the universe? Is our consciousness a phenomenon of biochemistry, an end product of evolutionary forces? Or is there a purpose to our existence, a reason why we're here experiencing the beauty and pain of physical life? How could our consciousness and the unfolding story of each of our lives have any significance against the vastness of space and time?

There is also the mystery of the universe itself: What is it? Where did it come from? Quantum physics tells us that matter is almost entirely empty space, with the movement of subatomic particles influenced by conscious observation. What seems solid is mostly empty, with tiny, spinning particles powered by an energy force we don't understand. Some nondual spiritual traditions have gone so far as to suggest that none of this is *really* real, including our own bodies and consciousness, and that they are states of illusion generated by karma. In Hinduism, the universe is just thought, a dream in the mind of Brahma. And our consciousness, our lives, are just a part of that dream. Many indigenous traditions operate on different discrete borderlines between pure dream and pure reality or Dreamtimes.

Religions and spiritual traditions have created complex cosmologies to answer the questions: Why are we here? What is this place? Some believe we are here to be tested, to be saved or shown worthy. Some believe we are created and placed here to worship God, to keep him from being alone, or to reflect his own nature to him. Others contend that souls incarnate, over and over, to learn and evolve. And their versions of God learn and evolve with them. There are also traditions that suggest we are all one consciousness, that souls may individuate briefly only to return to the sea of collective consciousness.

These cosmologies describe very different pictures of the spirit world: sitting on clouds playing harps; contemplating the face of God; having continuous access to gustatory and sexual pleasure; living as kings or laborers or slaves (whatever status one achieved on Earth); joining ancestors, guides, or spirit animals; passing through bardos that test souls and provide new lessons; descending to burn in eternal punishment; joining soul groups while continuing to learn and develop spiritual careers; and many, many other visions of the afterlife. Every religion or wisdom tradition tells us absolutely that their version of a soul's purpose and destiny is true.

In the face of so many conflicting narratives, are there any pathways to truth that we might find? Is there a truth within us that we could discover—something that grows from the wisdom of our own soul?

This guided journal is about discovering your soul's answers to the twin questions: Why are we here? What is this place? Each chapter provides guidance from the spirit world followed by a prompt to help you unlock your soul's own wisdom and truth. To respond to these prompts, you can use Deep Knowledge Meditation, a process that will help you uncover your own sense of what's real (see page 10 for instructions).

GUIDANCE FROM THE SPIRIT WORLD

Who is better able to describe the mysteries of life, death, and destiny than someone who has already died? The guidance in this book comes from Jordan, my son, a young man when he died in 2008 and who has since channeled three books describing the afterlife and our mission on this planet (*Seeking Jordan*, *The Luminous Landscape of the Afterlife*, and *Love in the Time of Impermanence*). Jordan's observations, which are shown in italic on left-hand pages, are a beginning, a launching place for your own journey of self-exploration; they are not something you're encouraged to accept and buy into. Their purpose is to allow you to begin a conversation with your own soul, a quest for your own truth. That's where the prompts come in. On the pages facing Jordan's observations you will find a page of prompts. These prompts appear on a background of sky and mountains. They are offered to help you explore the topics Jordan presents more deeply, using the technique of Deep Knowledge Meditation.

My Search for Jordan

Jordan died when he was twenty-three. Four men attempted to steal the bike he was riding home from work. There was a furious physical battle, and when they couldn't subdue him, they shot him.

At the time, Jordan was in the early stages of a career in computer animation; he lived with his girlfriend, played serious guitar, and showered everyone with his keen, irreverent humor. Jordan was, in other ways, unremarkable—just another young man dead on the streets of San Francisco. But he was so much more than simple demographics and descriptors. Those who knew him felt held by a powerful force—his love, care, and unfailing support. What's remarkable is that didn't stop with his death. If anything, the power of Jordan's former ego identity as well as his spirit has strengthened rather than faded as he continues to love, guide, and hold us from the afterlife.

I began instinctively searching for Jordan, and he started reaching out to me, within a few weeks of his death. My own scientific, evidence-based belief system vied with my intuition and innate clairsentience as Jordan began showing up in my dreams and the dreams of others—sometimes with messages for his mother and me. He made himself known in waking visions (once for me and for several others), as well as through messages from mediums, musicians, and psychically attuned friends.

I underwent a past-life hypnotic regression, that, bizarre as it initially seemed, revealed Jordan to have been my wife in a nineteenth-century seaside village and offered glimpses of various shared lives stretching back to the Middle Ages. Following my death (as a book-binder) in that village, I entered the life-between-lives and heard briefly from Jordan about lessons learned and unlearned in the life of the bookmaker and what I've agreed to work on in my current life.

Nine months after Jordan's death, I consulted psychologist Allan Botkin, who had developed a way to adapt

Eye Movement Desensitization and Reprocessing (EMDR, a more general modality for treating trauma) to facilitate communication with the dead. He called it Induced After-Death Communication (IADC), and during the process I heard Jordan's voice for the first time since he was killed. It was clearly, unmistakably him; he said he was happy and continued to watch over his mother and me.

The heavy stones of grief lifted a bit: Jordan still existed; his love continued to be a force in our world. I could feel it. But all of our communications continued to be one-way. Jordan could send me messages—clear and direct—and I could receive them. I could feel his love in my body, and receive, at times, his guidance. But we couldn't converse—ask and answer questions—as we had for so many years around the kitchen table.

The need to talk—to ask questions and receive answers—powered the next phase of my search. About a year after Jordan's death, I consulted the late Ralph Metzner, a specialist in after-death communication. Metzner said—and this made the greatest impression on me—that Jordan, and anyone in spirit, is just a thought away. As soon as the mind recalls that person, the channel opens between the physical plane and that soul in the afterlife. I was affirmed, inspired, and changed by what Metzner said. It was new and, at the same time, something I had always known. It ignited in me the hope that Jordan and I could have real conversations. Not just about our shared experiences, or guidance for how best to live out my life as Matthew, but descriptions of the afterlife, a reason why we come to this planet, a glimpse at the greater reality that comprises the universe and the forces that shaped it.

In sharing his wisdom, Metzner gave me the greatest gift I've ever received—the ability to communicate at will with the dead. He did this very simply and in a single hour of instruction. The channeling process is described in the appendix to this book; I have taught it to hundreds of people, and most report success communicating to souls in spirit.

Channeling, as I learned to practice it, starts with a breath-based meditation and culminates in a question that is written down and directed to a specific soul in spirit. The answer—which can arrive as a halting phrase, a pressured string of words, or a download of "knowing"—should also be written down. After digesting the answer, one can ask another question.

Immediately, on that first night after Metzner taught me to channel, I had my first conversation with Jordan. It was his voice (inside of me), his way of talking, and he was telling me things I'd never thought of or dreamt. I filled several pages with questions and answers. I thanked him and could feel his love filling my body. Over the years we've had hundreds of conversations. In response to my questions, Jordan has described the following:

- what to expect in the early stages after transition (death)
- what souls do in the afterlife
- how to prepare for death
- the nature of time
- why we incarnate to physical worlds
- how we learn through experiences of pain and loss
- how love is a gravitational force holding the physical and spirit worlds together
- why souls exist—our purpose
- the origin of matter and energy
- the nature of the Divine

Our conversations have revealed so much and given such important guidance that Jordan urged that they be made available to others. This book is a result.

Jordan was my son. But he is also a spirit who has lived many lives, and who, in the afterlife, continues to guide me and many thousands of others. He has his own answers to the mystery of our life, but they are not absolute. They are a trailhead for *your* journey. A place to begin your search for your own soul's truth.

WHY THIS JOURNAL IS FOR YOU

I have a picture on my wall of enslaved people picking cotton on a plantation. I keep it to remind me of the suffering, exploitation, and profound inequities experienced on this planet. I mention this not to suggest acceptance for all the suffering that continues around us but to remember that we face so much pain in this life. Our role and work here is a special mission. Jordan will describe his understanding of that mission, the reason for all our challenges, losses, and struggles. But you are on the same journey as Jordan, and me, and so many souls who come here to learn.

Look inside. Listen to the guidance you receive from reflecting on the prompts. The answers are within.

DEEP KNOWLEDGE MEDITATION

There are many forms of meditation designed for a myriad of purposes. The goal of Deep Knowledge Meditation* is to unleash unconscious and intuitive wisdom that has accumulated over multiple lifetimes and is held in the awareness of each soul.

Our conscious recall, what we can access from working memory, is limited to what serves us to survive. But our deepest knowledge, what we have gained from thousands of choices, losses, mistakes, and moments of love over our many incarnations, is a north star pointing us to what matters, to how we can navigate life on this planet.

---

*This term and the meditation itself first appeared in my book with Jeffrey C. Wood titled *The New Happiness.*

How to Practice
Deep Knowledge Meditation

Deep Knowledge Meditation starts with a question, something you want to know or understand. After you read the guidance from Jordan, settle into your own inquiry. Prepare to listen for what you seek to know. You will find the meditation prompts indicated by the same background image used on this page.

Now focus on your breath, bringing your attention to your diaphragm, the center of life and breath. On each in-breath, say to yourself "in," and on each out-breath say to yourself "out." Keep saying "in" and "out" with your breath. "In" . . . and "out." "In" . . . and "out." And when thoughts arise, just note the thought to yourself—*there's a thought*—and gently return your attention to your breath, observing the source of life.

And now, in the space between breaths, between thoughts, gently return to the question. What is it you want to know and understand? Listen for your own truth and wisdom. Wait for your deep intuition to answer. It may come in the form of an image or picture or in the form of a few focused words. It may come as a download of knowledge that you might need to sort through and find language to describe. It may show up as just "knowing," a deep sense of what is true.

However the answer arrives, give it room to coalesce in your awareness. *Feel* it without trying to press it into any idea in particular. There is no rush to knowing. Your truth lives inside as a light that shines from all of your experience and all of your living.

After each prompt, if you are moved to explore the topic more profoundly, do Deep Knowledge Meditation. Listen to your heart and all of your accumulated wisdom. And then begin journaling what comes up. Your feelings. Your hopes and wishes. Your thoughts and sense of truth. Pause and make room for all of it. There is no right or wrong; there is only your deepest wisdom, what your soul has learned over its many lives.

Repeat the process of Deep Knowledge Meditation for each prompt that you react to, each thought that summons in you a sense of inquiry, of wanting to know more.

Remember that what Jordan says is just a start, a place to begin your own process of discovery. Let the questions germinate and open your mind. The truth is in you; it is in each individual soul.

Your journaled answers are a record of your own sense of what is. Perhaps they will evolve as you learn during this lifetime and as you return to the prompts again and again. These are your answers to the great questions: Why are we here? What is this place?

. . . .

1

What Is All, the Divine, God?

ALL, THE FIRST CONSCIOUSNESS, has not always existed. But it is now eternal and ever evolving. The work of All is to create and then to learn from everything it has created.

All is God but not the conventional idea of God—a perfect, all-powerful entity that created and is the prime cause of all events on Earth.

All created the material universe—including Earth and countless other planets on which souls incarnate. But All is neither perfect nor all-powerful. All is learning and evolving. All constantly grows in knowledge and awareness, and much of what All learns comes from us—souls who incarnate into the physical universe.

∼ All's Limited Power ∼

All lacks the power to create perfection, or to know what, at any given moment, is unknown. As the consciousness of All grows, it increasingly penetrates and occupies the dark unknown. But there will always be dark places that the consciousness of All—while ever expanding— has not reached.

The idea that All is the puppet master, pulling strings to create each change, each event on Earth, is false. The consciousness of All creates matter and the laws of the material universe but then releases the universe to evolve according to physical laws and the law of cause and effect.

Life develops on some planets and can evolve to higher levels of consciousness. As certain species evolve a capacity for memory and abstract thought, All permits souls to incarnate in these worlds and physical bodies. The purpose is to learn, at a micro level of experience and interaction, what the mind of All can not discern. All is like a father, too big to enter a playhouse, listening to the child describe what it's like to be inside.

All doesn't control events; All observes and learns from them. All creates the conditions on each planet but gives incarnating souls free will to respond to them. Each thing we do in response to the challenges of our lives teaches All lessons it could not possibly learn otherwise.

Jordan suggests that All, God, sets the universe in motion but doesn't exert control over the events of our lives. Rather, God's role is to observe and learn from everything that happens.

How does this fit with your relationship to God?

Do you experience God helping you to confront life's challenges?

If you do, what does that experience feel like?

Does your experience of God feel like support or does it feel like active intervention to change events?

· ·

∼ Devotion to All, the Divine, God ∼

*The devout are sure, and they are held in a net of absolute.
Their certainty diminishes fear. But the cost is openness to
truth and the joy of discovery.*

*Being devout means two things—belief in a set of principles for
living, and devotion to a strong, protective deity. Being devout
is a form of spirituality in which the rules of life are given to
you (think Ten Commandments), and an all-powerful deity
offers help with the pain and struggle of living (if you offer back
enough worship, sacrifice, and supplication).*

*A spirituality of devotion provides a structure and a sense of
security. But what it cannot do is bring you closer to the truth
or the web of love that surrounds you. There is no room for
discovery of your own growing wisdom or the many voices of
consciousness that can support and guide you. You are alone with
your God instead of one with All, with every conscious entity.*

*The difference between devotion and spirituality is a sense
of struggling alone (with your God) verses belonging and
being held by the love of All. True safety can only be found
in the immortal relationships with every soul we love and by
belonging to All. It cannot be found in the intersessions of
some God to fix things that go wrong on Earth.*

*As spirituality grows beyond devotion and religion, the soul
is liberated to be God, to belong to All, to do what it was
made to do, which is learn.*

What is the role of worship, praise, and asking
the Divine for help with our problems?

Where does God end and we begin?
. . . .

∼ We Are All ∼

All—collective consciousness or God—includes every individual soul incarnating on planets throughout the universe. We are All, and the consciousness of All holds us. We were created to help All evolve. Everything we see, know, and learn, everything we feel and experience, is held in the mind of All. Just as every leaf is individual and also part of the tree, we are individual bits of consciousness simultaneously joined in the mind of All.

So we can never separate from All; we can never be judged and cast out. We can never lose our relationship to All because we are All. We cannot stop serving All because we will never stop learning and bringing what we learn to the mind of All.

∿ There Is No Judgment, No Good or Bad ∿

All isn't good or bad; All just is. And no soul is good or bad. A soul just is. The idea of an all good and perfect deity testing each soul's worthiness of eternal life is wrong. Was the entire universe—every galaxy, nebula, black hole, and star—made so All can evaluate Homo sapiens *on one small world? Reason tells us this can't be true. But it's also wrong because on the deepest level God and every soul are* the same thing. *They cannot be separated.*

The mere thought that there is good and evil creates evil, *the means by which we separate ourselves from each other. Reject the other. Dehumanize the other. Separation—the delusion that we are not one—is what evil is made of.*

How does judgment—deciding if we are
good or bad—square with the role
God serves in your life?

Why does evil exist in the world?
What would it take to get rid of evil?
. . . .

∼ How Judgment Hurts Us ∼

All doesn't judge, nor do spirits in the afterlife. Only humans do. The compulsion to judge dates back to members of the tribe being good and worthy. Anyone else was foreign, subhuman—someone who could be killed, stolen from, or enslaved, or someone who could kill, steal from, or enslave us.

Religions often encouraged good–bad judgments. If you follow the rules and are good, you are rewarded with the promise of paradise and belonging to the faithful on Earth. If you break the rules, you are cast out.

Judgment is always about casting out, separating, and losing our connection to each other. It is the antithesis of love because it refuses to recognize our oneness, our belonging to All. Violence and war are the ultimate outcome of judgment, as is divorce, child abuse, and nearly every form of cruelty. When you judge someone as bad, you are set free to inflict any harm, any "punishment." You are free to throw them away. Judgment sticks a knife in our love—even when we judge ourselves, we strip away all compassion, all caring for our humanness. We separate from ourselves. We throw ourselves away.

Our spiritual work on this planet is to rise above judgment to love everyone and everything, even the ones who hurt us—all the flaws and broken places, all the pain and failed ways we try to fix the pain, all the mistakes and differences. Learning not to judge is a first step to spiritual awakening.

What is the role of judgment—discovering if others are good or evil—in our lives?

What effect does judgment have on our relationships?

What effect does judgment have on love?
. . . .

∼ One Consciousness ∼

Each object, each living being is the work of consciousness. Each object and being has the awareness of the consciousness that created it. It is all one experience, located differently. Just like the experience of your head and foot is one experience, located differently.

Becoming aware of the one experience can create a deep sense of peace and belonging. We belong together as one consciousness but experience this from separate locations, from separate vantage points and perspectives.

Everything is an expression of the one consciousness, the one awareness. The one consciousness watches from billions of positions, seeing simultaneously through billions of different windows. Yet what it is aware of and sees from every position is one.

Jordan suggests that we are part of one consciousness, located in the individual awareness of each soul. He goes further— saying that each object created by All holds the consciousness of God within it.

What connection do you feel to every object, every living thing, every soul—around you?

What is that connects you to everything outside yourself?

....

∼ How All Creates ∼

Everything we touch, everything we are, is the energy of thought. Thoughts are finite and transient. But the mind of All that thinks them is eternal. Each thought is part of the evolution of All (God, collective consciousness). Each thought has the power to create extensions of consciousness (individual souls) or new environments (planets, or the universe, itself) in which consciousness can learn and grow.

Consciousness imagines. This imagining looks beyond what is to what could be, beyond the limits of the current reality to the next world. So imagination, the picture of what could be, is the birth of the universe. It is everything that drives All forward.

As All imagines something, energy collects around the idea, taking the shape of the imagined object or entity. Imagination is thus the source of matter. If All imagines a soul, conscious energy congeals around this new identity. If All imagines an object bound by certain laws of physics, energy organizes subatomically to create a lattice structure on which to build mass of a certain shape and density. Energy always responds to and is shaped by conscious thought—whether it is an electron responding to observations or the spinning arms of galaxies driven by an intention in the mind of All.

What role do the thoughts of All serve in creating the world we know?

What does your own knowledge and wisdom tell you about how the universe was shaped?

In what ways do thoughts have the power to create what we see?

· ·

∼ Why All Creates ∼

All is a single consciousness that holds everything. Both the material world and spirit world exist because they were created by All and are held in the mind of All.

All creates to express in form something it has conceived and imagined. Then All animates its creations with natural laws (in the case of energy and matter) or consciousness and free will (in the case of souls). All observes as its creations evolve, and All learns from them. And as All watches the universe and souls who interact with it, All evolves— has new knowledge and thinks new things.

So All creates for three reasons: for the pleasure of conceiving something new and beautiful, to enter into relationship with what was created, and to learn and grow from observing its creation.

All will continue to create forever because it is the means by which All evolves. With each creation the mind of All expands to hold a new thought. And as each creation evolves, All watches and learns.

If there is a God, why would it create? Why would it make a material universe?

From where or what did you come?

Who or what were you created by?
....

~ How Consciousness Uses Matter ~

Consciousness, All, watches the workings of matter in much the same way people watch fish swimming in a tank, observing the endless movement, the changes, the surprising and unique behaviors. Or how bird watchers observe the plumage, flight, call patterns, and nesting behaviors of a particular species. Or how scientists watch the behavior of electrons when these are inflamed by conscious thought.

The material universe is an endless sea of phenomena for consciousness to observe and learn from. Consciousness uses matter in the same way children learn about the properties and functional possibilities of their toys. A child arranges plastic soldiers on a battlefield, assigning real and imagined functions. One toy soldier stands at a gate (in reality) and guards a miniature fortress (in imagination). In the mind of All there is no difference between reality and imagination. What All imagines becomes material and real.

Jordan says that consciousness, All, observes matter and uses it to learn. How do you learn?

How useful is it to you to learn through observation—from watching how events unfold, watching the story of what happens?

How do you learn from the material phenomena that surround you?

. . . .

2

The Nature
of Matter and
Energy

ENERGY IS THE SOURCE of consciousness and the material universe. There was a time when *what is* did not include consciousness—there was only energy.

Undifferentiated energy was the source of the first self-aware consciousness (what would become All), in much the same way amino acids, arranged in unique formations, were the progenitors of physical life. So energy existed first—before consciousness and before a material universe. Energy is the *first cause*, igniting everything that followed.

Primal, undifferentiated energy inhabits the empty dark. There it is mere potential, and potential is a force. Energy has a built-in bias, a destiny to become more and more complex. In many ways, this is the first law of existence (reality).

Energy has always filled the void. It existed long before matter and is therefore independent of matter. Energy is the *potential* for heat, movement, light, and thought, but primal energy is none of those things. It is *no thing*. It is like a charge stored in a battery—merely something *there* waiting to be harnessed, waiting to become light, heat, matter, and of course thought.

Energy arises from all the infinite possibilities of what can fill the void. The void requires, in fact creates, the counterforce of energy. The void demands something to fill it in the same way a vacuum seeks something of higher density to fill its nothingness. The requirement is like an unfelt wind—not of particles, but a potential, a foreshadowing of what, by necessity, must inevitably be.

Even in its primal state, energy's sole intention is to fill the void. At first with mere potential, and then, over time with heat, movement, light, thought, and matter. The emptiness of the void ignites primal energy because its nothingness is inherently unstable. Energy is a natural response or consequence of the void.

∼ Primal Energy Is a Form of Waiting ∼

Consider the experience of waiting for a train. The track is empty, disappearing into the distance. Before there is a train there is tension, an energy field of no-train. *There is a similar tension and energy field in* no-thing. *There is a waiting—the power of* no-thing *demanding something. That energy potential is the beginning of everything.*

What things in your life have you waited for while acutely feeling their absence?

How have you experienced the tension of *no-thing*, a void that demanded that you do something to fill it?

Where does all the energy in the universe come from?

· ·

∼ Primal Energy Is the Source of Consciousness ∼

As energy evolved toward primitive versions of photons—the particles that comprise light—it not only pierced the dark void but also developed the capacity to observe. Light, having the capacity to observe, is consciousness, which ultimately has the capacity to reflect, to know. Thus light—seeing and knowing—is the fundamental building block of consciousness. Here's how light became conscious.

In the beginning, light was just energy manifesting itself—a force becoming something out of the void. But, because energy must evolve to more complex forms, light started to do more than glow. It began to illuminate the only thing then in existence—itself. At that moment a new tension arose. This new object in the void—self-illumined light— was unconscious. Yet its existence needed to be seen for it to evolve further. It needed to know itself. In this first, primitive moment of awareness, light recognized light. Light saw light. Light became conscious.

Illumination is the necessary prerequisite and product of seeing and knowing. When we speak of casting light on a subject, we mean focusing the full awareness of consciousness on a phenomenon until it shines, clearly and intensely, out from the void of the unknown.

Jordan suggests that light is the origin
of consciousness. And that light became
conscious when it began to see
and know itself.

What is the most important work of
your consciousness?

What does it seek to know? Yourself? The world
around you? Deeper nonphysical realities? Is it
helping you survive? Something else?

· ·

∼ The Vast Sea of the Universe ∼

*We are floating on what's real. It supports us and creates
our context. We live in boats on the vast sea of the universe,
deluded that we are alone while we are all one with the
thought that created everything.*

*Consciousness is what we are and what we float in.
Consciousness is the sea, the boat, and the perspective
of the individual sojourner.*

*Beneath the apparent universe, like a scaffolding of support,
is a matrix of thought energy. And beneath that is the whole
of consciousness and its intention to create and evolve.
The energy scaffolding of the material universe creates
subatomic motion (which produces light and heat). So
everything that surrounds us is a manifestation of thought,
which generates motion, light, and heat.*

Examine your own sense of truth. What
created and maintains the universe?

How might the universe be one thing—
thought—and also held together by natural
laws governing matter and energy?

What is your understanding of the "scaffolding"
that supports everything we see and know?
....

∼ The Relationship between Matter and Energy ∼

Matter is energy expressed in a different form. Matter and energy are interchangeable. There are infinite forms that matter and energy can take—just as there are infinite forms that a sculptor with a chisel can extract from a block of granite. Energy is what makes particles move from the hidden, dark places to be lit and seen briefly at the surface of the matrix. And it is energy that makes these particles disappear, to become undetectable and nonspecific again. Matter appears and disappears, becoming heat and light and movement when it appears and then sinking back into the sea of undifferentiated energy.

So energy rises above the threshold of visibility to become particles and in time sinks below that line to disappear, undetected, into the energy field again. This cycle continues, governed by the intentions of consciousness rather than laws of particle physics. Consciousness causes energy to shift into particle and material form or back to energy again. The border between energy and matter is porous, but when matter slips across the boundary—back into the energy field—there is a sudden expansion, an explosion of energy. The opposite is also true. All, God, can decide, at some point, to shift energy into mass exponentially and give birth to a new universe, such as what happened with the big bang.

Jordan suggests that energy rises to become visible in the form of subatomic particles, which then become physical mass: the planets and stars, everything we can see and touch. But all of matter can turn back again into an invisible energy field. This forms the platform for the impermanent, ever-changing nature of reality.

How do you notice the impermanence of the physical world?

How does the impermanence of the physical world feel? How does it affect you?

. . . .

3

The Nature
of a Soul

THE ONE CONSCIOUSNESS—All—created the universe in which to learn. But there were limits to what it could learn as an observer. So All created smaller units of consciousness—souls—to enter and interact with its universe. Each soul has awareness, memory, the capacity to choose, and the ability to conceptualize, feel, and love. Every function of souls, every ability is in the service of learning. Learning is the soul's purpose, and it is a sacred, unswerving mission. Souls cope with every vicissitude—illness, loss, survival needs, overwhelming impulses and emotions, desire, social and interpersonal struggles, the forces of nature, threats in every form, physical and emotional pain, and the endless friction of coping with an impermanent world. Souls learn how to live in the physical world but also how to love in it. And how to find and make beauty—another form of love— in every moment.

Each soul has an identity—which is essentially everything it has learned in its existence. But each soul also belongs to All, remains a part of the one consciousness— the collective awareness that includes all things.

∼ What Souls Learn Lasts Forever ∼

*Everything we learn as souls—both in the physical universe
and the spirit world—stays with us forever. Our knowledge
and wisdom continue to deepen. And everything
we learn becomes part of the knowledge
and continuing evolution of All.*

*In each lifetime, we are like bees venturing out from
the hive of spirit. Instead of nectar, we collect knowledge and
wisdom. We learn. And what we learn we share with All.
This is our purpose, our work.*

What does it feel like your purpose might be for coming here and living this life?

If our work as souls is to learn, what have you learned in this life?

What are you learning currently? What might you have left to learn?

. . . .

∼ The Physical Challenges
of Incarnation ∼

Earth and the human body are notoriously challenging.
Young souls, in their first incarnations, struggle to master
and control the bodies they enter. The nervous and limbic
(emotional) systems can be highly reactive. Cravings for
pleasure, substances, and sexual desire can overwhelm the
soul's efforts to control and direct the human body.

How do you struggle to master and
control your body?

What urges do you struggle with?

What ways have you learned to
help you control them?
. . . .

∼ Overcoming the Urge to "Other" ∼

The hard-wired bias toward tribalism divides the world into good (us) and bad (them). Destructive urges to attack the bad "other" are especially difficult to manage for young souls. A mere thought that labels someone as "bad" is often enough to unleash anger and a desire to punish or attack. Good–bad judgments dehumanize, disconnect, and are the main source of evil.

On Earth, we have to learn how to love in the face of each of these challenges.

Do you find yourself dividing people or things into what's good or bad?

How does this affect your relationships? Your emotional life?

If you make good–bad judgments about yourself, how do they affect you?

....

~ A Soul's Missions ~

As a soul prepares to incarnate, there are always two missions. The first mission is how to love while encountering loss, hurt, and adversity on the physical plane. The second mission is more specific and personal for each soul. This may include certain unlearned lessons from previous lives—things like patience, acceptance, courage, caring, commitment, fortitude—values that the soul continues to work on. Or it may be learning the means to navigate and face particular challenges. The soul's personal mission often includes specific goals for what the soul will do or create in this lifetime.

We come to our lives and our planet with a clear lesson plan. Even when we fail, we accomplish the most important thing—to learn. But often, in crucial moments during incarnate life, we make choices that may be new, that push us past old, limited patterns. And it is then we feel a spiritual peace, a rightness that reminds us of why we came here.

When in your life have you learned how to love while encountering loss, hurt, or adversity?

What lessons are showing up for you in this life?

What might be unlearned lessons from previous lives that you are learning about in this life?

What do you think you were meant to do or achieve while here?

When in your life have you made a choice that pushed you beyond old, limited patterns? How did you feel after you made that choice?

. . . .

∼ Lessons from Choices ∼

*This world is a playing field on which to make choices.
There is no choice but to choose. We are here to watch each
moment and choose what to do in response.*

*Guides and loved ones on the other side whisper their
support to help us navigate. But we must encounter the
outcomes from our choices alone. Pain and spiritual
contentment are the two major outcomes of choosing; they
are how we learn from what we choose.*

*The capacity to choose is the cornerstone of what is real;
we live at the epicenter of the moment. Reality unfolds with
each of our actions, our choices, to become the next moment.
Every choice makes something happen and opens the door
to the next reality. And everything that happens leads to the
next choice. The weight of this responsibility—to propel the
present from one moment to the next—is enormous
for each soul.*

*This is the deepest truth about time in the physical realm
as experienced by embodied consciousness. You create what
is real from moment to moment, and you can't escape that
burden until death. The "moment" is what's real.*

What are the most important choices you've
made in your life?

What did you learn from them?

How did each of these choices open the door
to the next reality?

If your choices are how you create your reality,
your life, which types of choices—large and
singular or small and frequent—have most
shaped your life?

. . . .

∼ Lessons Only Possible
in Incarnate Life ∼

*In the place between lives, the soul remembers the lessons
of each existence and the love of All. But we forget most of
what we knew as immortal souls when we come to Earth,
and we are born with no memory of our lives in spirit.
And yet it is incarnate life, the not knowing, that makes it
possible for us to awaken.*

*In the amnesia of life is a beautiful opportunity, a painful
aloneness, an emptiness that permits learning that's
unencumbered by everything we knew before. It's a pristine
field without hills or promontories; it is a place where
everything is new, unblemished by past experience. Here we
see light—not of the galaxies, not of history and all that has
passed, but the light of the moment lived, of the pain or joy,
of time held and illuminated by a single experience.*

*This is why we must have reverence for life and why it is
precious. Nowhere in the heavens of the spirit world are
the lessons of this incarnate life possible. If we remembered
where we came from and what we knew there,
we wouldn't take seriously the challenges and
choices we face on this planet.*

What are moments when life has felt precious?

What did you learn from these moments?

Have you ever felt a sense of lessons from past
lives or knowledge from the spirit world?
What did you know?

. . . .

∿ Lessons of Love ∿

In the spirit world love unites all. The truth that we are All and are united by love is the central experience of Spirit.

We enter the physical world to find that same truth, as opposed to merely having that truth surround us. The truth you arrive at, the truth you discover on Earth, makes the light of love burn brighter. On Earth that truth is earned over millennia through the struggles and learned wisdom of billions of souls. It is polished by striving, by the pain of loss and the collapse of civilizations. It is polished by each act of love, each step beyond the boundary of self, until it is a brilliant light that can be seen by All, until it is a light that is All.

So we are not here merely to learn what is already known; we are here to create a new truth and in doing so make it brighter than all the light in the universe.

One way to understand this is through the metaphor of the perfect family. If you are a child in a perfect family, you'd grow up surrounded by love and support. You'd live at peace, completely taken care of. Then you'd grow up, go out into the world, and try to make a family like that yourself. You'd face pain and obstacles trying to love, support, and protect your family. And in doing so, you'd learn more about what love is and what it really takes for children to be held—safe and protected. We come to Earth, therefore, not to rediscover old truths but to actually create them ourselves.

Jordan suggests that we come here to learn
new truths about how to create and give love.

As you look back on your life, how have you
found new ways to give and express love?

What have you learned about love?

How have you experienced someone else
creating love?

What experiences or opportunities might you
have in the future where you could create love?

~ Lessons from Experience ~

A soul is a unit of consciousness—simultaneously separate and a part of All. There are many forms of consciousness. Flies have consciousness. Boa constrictors have consciousness. But they don't remain separate consciousnesses after death. The mind of All learns how the fly and boa constrictor consciousness experiences the world, but they, at their level of awareness, are incapable of conceptual learning. They are subsumed back into the mind of All at death.

Human soul consciousness, in contrast, is capable of abstract thought and learning. It learns and evolves as it interacts with the physical environment, and it learns in relationship to other souls and forms of consciousness in both the spirit world and here on Earth. Soul consciousness can interact with the physical universe in ways that All cannot. Soul consciousness can form relationships with objects, places, and other souls—learning from each connection—in ways that the mind of All would engulf, for it would be too big and charged with energy to participate in these micro level entanglements. For example, All can only conceptually experience orgasm, while an embodied soul can fully feel the experience as a physical entity. All can only conceptually experience loss through death, whereas a soul, consumed with pain at the moment of loss, can teach All the severing nature of loss and how it can be faced.

In essence, soul consciousness exists, and will continue to exist, to learn and to give All everything it has learned.

Jordan says we can learn important things from our interactions with the physical world that All cannot; that All can only conceptually understand what we learn from direct experience.

When have you sensed that the things you learn seem to be shared with something outside yourself?

When you look into your own experience, what knowledge have you given to All?

. . . .

∼ Pain in the Material World ∼

Pain is ubiquitous in the material world. We collide with things—physically and emotionally—that hurt us.

Souls come to the physical plane because of what pain can teach. There is no pain in the spirit world. No yearning, no hurt or loss. So we come here to learn what happens when we fail to act with love.

Consider the father who slaps his son over and over and discovers that the boy won't speak to him. This is one way pain teaches. Not just in this life but in the next and next as we carry these lessons forward—if we don't learn from them and evolve. This man hurts people, so his boy will not speak to him, perhaps the man's wife gives up and leaves, or his friend is no longer his friend. This is how souls grow: from hard lessons they could only learn here and then carry forever.

What have you learned from the pain you've faced in this life?

What things have you done or which choices have you made that had a painful outcome, and yet you learned from them?

What is a lesson you've learned in this life that you hope to carry into the next?

....

4

Love and Entanglement

LOVE AND ENTANGLEMENT are the same force. They hold all of us together in both the physical and spirit worlds. This is because once joined, subatomic particles retain an eternal relationship. Though they may scatter around the universe, they remain entangled, and one will react to whatever affects the other. Remember, this is also how we remain connected to All.

Souls are entangled in precisely the same way: once connected by love, they remain entangled forever. What affects one affects the other. What one learns becomes wisdom shared with the other. What one needs or feels is felt by the other. Soul entanglement cannot be broken or lost.

~ Gravity ~

The gravity of love is nothing more than attention, seeing. What consciousness sees, it binds and holds and entangles with love. The mind of All is in constant meditation, observing and holding everything it has created, every real thing. Thus, because All sees all, All loves all.

Conscious attention is love, seeing is love, knowing is love—the energy that binds everything. The more clearly consciousness sees, the more deeply consciousness knows, the more intense is the holding force of love.

Gravity is love, the affinity things have for each other. Everything is entangled and held by the gravity of love.

This same gravity of love holds the spirit world together and all the individual souls who populate it. Gravity allows souls to merge in small groups or into All. Merging is just a letting go—a falling—into the gravitational force of love.

Everything is in relationship to everything else. The gravitational force of love is what makes and maintains that relationship. Our feet press against the Earth because of love. Worlds fly around suns because of love. Each spinning galaxy holds each star—each brilliant flash and product of consciousness—in love's gravity.

Jordan suggests that love, the gravitational force that connects everything, is a product of attention. What we see and know, we come to love. Love becomes a gravitational force that holds us in relationship.

What connects you to the people and things that surround you?

What is the force that holds everything in your life, everything that matters to you, together?

What does the energy of love—gravity—need from you in order to be sustained?

....

∼ Entanglement ∼

*In the same way we continue to love friends and relatives
in a distant town or country, souls who love are eternally
joined—no matter what. Though separated by space, anger,
abandonment, loss, or death, they are spiritually inseparable.
No force can break them apart.*

*Entanglement is a form of consciousness, of knowing, of
seeing the eternal light that joins us in relationship.*

Entanglement is the eternal connection that can form between souls. Despite appearances (abandonment) or harsh events (rejection), Jordan suggests that once entangled by love, we are forever connected.

For people and things you lost but once loved, does any part of the bond remain? How do you know? How do you experience the bond?

∼ Entanglement and the "Other" ∼

*Because we are all part of the same consciousness,
the same energy, when we see one another, we can
recognize the other as part of ourselves.*

*Entanglement is belonging; it is recognition of the other as
part of self. Other and self are the same. When we judge
we break relationship (entanglement). We separate and
unwittingly support evil. Love in the form of seeing,
knowing, showing compassion, and caring establishes
relationship and joins us as one.*

Looking back on the life you've lived so far, who is someone you judged as "other" who you now recognize in yourself?

How have judgments affected you?

How can we rid the world of disconnection (evil)?

. . . .

~ Entanglement and Nonduality ~

*Entanglement implies a universe that is both dual and
nondual: dual in the sense that entangled particles can have
separate locations, velocities, and vectors; but nondual in
the sense that they remain inextricably together—one. This
is the paradox of all reality. Trees on either side of a large
forest are both individual trees and a single entity of forest.
They are one with the forest and yet also an individual tree.
A carbon atom in a tall redwood is both the tree and a
particular atom, of which there are trillions in the redwood.
The appearance of separation is just one way
the whole is manifested.*

How do you feel part of something
beyond yourself?

If you feel connected to something outside
yourself, what is the force that holds you
together and in what ways do you
experience that force?

....

~ Love's Gravity Is the Center that Holds ~

All the individual parts of the physical universe fly apart; all the parts of the spirit world disseminate, seeking their own experiences and opportunities to learn. But a force holds everything in relationship. A force requires that they revolve and evolve around some center. The center does hold.

In the same way gravity holds planets in orbit around a sun, gravity holds the far-flung light of each individual consciousness near to the source, to All. Gravity is desire to stay close, to let no part be abandoned or fly away. It is the antithesis of loss. Gravity is the surrender of each individual part to relationship, to entanglement with every other part, with All.

What is your gravity, the center to your life
that holds you together?

How do you experience a sense of
"center," a connection to everything
that surrounds you?

·······································

5

Love on Earth

THERE ARE A HUNDRED WAYS to manifest love, which include healing, holding, protecting, validating, teaching, cleaning, beautifying, giving, joining, witnessing another's pain, caring and supporting in the face of pain, grieving, taking a blow meant for another, paying attention or seeing, surrendering, showing compassion, and many others. Many of these actions involve pain and sacrifice, and most of these forms teach lessons we could only learn in this painful place, yet all of them advance the conscious discovery of love.

~ Love in the Face of Pain ~

Everything we have and everything we know—
except our own and others' consciousness—is impermanent
and will be lost. How do we face impermanence?
How do we go on with life when the papier-mâché
elements of our world can break at any time? We go
on by seeing we are all captive to the same pain, the
same struggle, and the same losses, and by
giving our compassion to every soul
who suffers just like us.

Jordan suggests that compassion has its roots
in seeing the pain suffered by others.

What is your internal reaction when you
notice that others hurt?

How does the pain of another impact your
connection with them? Does their pain make you
feel more connected to them, or do you feel
disconnected, separated from their pain?

. . . .

~ Love, the Source of All Connection ~

Love is just a word. But it is the source of all connection; it is the power that unites every atom, every galaxy, and every soul to All. All consciousness is held together with love.

But love isn't just a passive state. For every incarnating soul, it is an active process of becoming. Souls discover how love changes relationships, how it evolves to extend our limited, tribal ideas of belonging.

Love helps us to grow in two ways in the material world. To begin, we learn what happens when we fail to love. We witness the pain and destruction in every relationship where love is forsaken, where it is abandoned in favor of desire or avoidance. We see what happens on Earth when choices are made empty of love, empty of care or compassion. The outcome of choices devoid of love leave us lost and alienated, crying out in a dark place where souls often wander alone. On the other hand, love is the source of all connection, and outcomes of choices made with love connect us to All.

The second way we grow on the physical plane is learning how to love when our emotions, our pain, and our needs all cry out for us to protect self, to ignore the other. Learning how to love when our distress and suffering demand that we sink into ego and self-focus is the great test of each lifetime. It is how we evolve from creatures bent on survival to souls fully aware of what connects us and binds us and allows us to belong to All.

What lessons have you learned when
something got in the way of your
ability to love?

What experiences have you had where you
had to push through some obstacle—a painful
emotion, some need or desire, or even
physical pain—in order to do what love
asked of you?

....

∼ To Love Everything ∼

Our goal on Earth is to see everything and to love everything.
And everything we learn to love expands us,
makes us more beautiful.

You can love what is ugly and deformed, what is without
apparent beauty. The person with the greatest damage is the
most important teacher of love. Loving this person is what
heals the juncture of light and dark, allowing you to see what
is ugly, what you don't like, with compassion.

In spirit, everything we see we know.
And everything we know, we love.

Souls in the afterlife understand something we only catch
hints of on Earth: there is nothing in the universe or the
world of spirit that can't be loved. It was all made of love; it
can all be seen and known, and it is all
held in the gravity of love.

Jordan suggests that learning to love what's broken or damaged is a pathway to deeper love. Truly seeing and knowing what has been hurt opens the door between souls.

What experiences have you had with difficult, damaged people (or even animals) that allowed you to see, know, and care for them?

How did your compassion and love for that person (or animal) impact your relationship with them?

. . . .

~ Love and Merging ~

Our dense physical form on Earth prevents us from merging with each other. So love must be an exchange of something passed between souls. Love must be expressed in words and touch that can't penetrate the inviolate boundary of the other. In the afterlife a soul's energy form isn't dense, but spacious. Souls can be permeable and merge, which allows a much deeper knowing, caring, and accepting than we can achieve on Earth.

When have you felt moments of merging, a dissolving of boundaries that opened a deeper love between you and another?

∼ Love and Attention ∼

Everything can be loved. Whatever we truly see, whatever we consciously attend to will be loved. Love grows from attention. If you pay attention to the street where you live, you will love that street. If you deeply observe the humans gathered at a bus stop, you will love them. If you touch a carving made by a craftsman long ago, you will love the carving and the one who made it. If you stare long enough at the moon or Milky Way, you will love it. If you let your consciousness expand to include every soul on the planet, now or ever, you will love them, and you will feel your kinship, your belonging to this place, and to each other. That which receives your attention you come to know, and that which you come to know you come to love.

At once you are yourself and everything you behold. You are both separate and one. From your small spot in the universe you can watch everything, join and know everything, and feel the essence, the nature, and the light of everything. Which is exactly what love is.

Attention, Jordan says, leads to knowing. And truly knowing leads to love.

When you pay deep attention to someone or something, what happens?

If you experience a growing sense of care, how does that shift your relationship?

Do you notice other changes
in the relationship?

· ·

6

Time and Impermanence

TIME IS A MEASURE of change. And change is at the root of impermanence—the loss of things as they once were. As painful as impermanence is, it is necessary to our growth and evolution as souls.

Impermanence in physical reality is one key to how consciousness grows. Without change and loss of things as they once were, there would be nothing for consciousness to respond to. There would be nothing to learn from. Stasis prevents growth. So impermanence, embedded as it is in the physical world, is our ticket to ride: to see, to respond to, and to learn from new things. Change and loss power revelation, becoming, and learning.

～ Time Is Beautiful ～

Time marks everything that changes, everything we are learning, and everything All is learning. Time is never empty. It is full of the evolution of consciousness. Earth time at some point will stop, but the time during which consciousness evolves will go on forever.

Celebrate time as you celebrate your own growth. Birthdays are celebrated because the individual is another year older and wiser. Each year teaches much about holding and being love in the face of pain, about what's most important. Even the failure to love—and its consequences—teaches much.

So time is a friend, even though it takes. Everything physical is impermanent. But time gives us something eternal and never lost—wisdom and the growth of consciousness. What time takes was never meant to last. What it gives lasts forever in each soul consciousness and in the mind of All.

Time can take things that matter to you. And it can give new wisdom and learning.

What is your emotional relationship to time? For example, does it frighten you, or does it point to a future you want to experience?

What does it mean to you that the material world was never meant to last?

. . . .

∼ Reality, Choices, and the Future ∼

While we can see the future of the species and this planet from the spirit world, that future could change depending on billions of individual decisions by souls occupying human bodies on Earth. So while the future is seen and known from the spirit world, it is plastic and can be rewritten depending on human choices.

How does it feel to consider that each
decision you make changes the future,
pushes it (and all who live in it) in
a different direction?

What future do you want your
decisions to create?
....

∼ When Time Stops ∼

Someday time will stop for the Earth—and for the universe itself. Time will stop because all change and movement will stop, and matter as form will return to mere energy. That energy, driven by the mind of All, will eventually take new material forms, such as a new, more beautiful, and more complex universe. At that moment, physical time will start again, beginning at the zero hour of the new big bang.

What does it feel like to contemplate time
stopping for this universe?

Does your wisdom and intuition tell you there
is only this universe and no other? Or does it
feel like the material universe could become
something else, something as yet unknown?

What do you think and feel about the
possibility of another, more evolved universe
that replaces this one?

If matter eventually returns to energy, and this
universe is eventually replaced by another, what
does that mean for consciousness? For All?
. . . .

∿ Impermanence and Reality ∿

All physical reality is subject to change and at some point will end. Whether it is a river that stops flowing, a star that burns out, or an entire universe collapsing back into the mind of All or God. Even in our brief lifetimes we observe these changes: a field paved over for development, a neighborhood with different stores, paint peeling on a once-bright façade, shoulders bent with age, or loved ones disappearing from the Earth.

Nothing can be forgotten or unlearned; these lessons will survive the species and the planet. The knowledge gained by incarnating souls—and by All—survives forever.

When you depart the Earth, will your
consciousness disappear, or will
your consciousness survive, continuing
to grow and evolve?

If all of physical reality changes and is
finally lost, what does that mean for you?
. . . .

～ Embracing Impermanence ～

All that we know is burning, being consumed. Reality is continually being lost, abandoned to the next instant of the timeline. In every moment consciousness is letting go of what's real, replacing it, after each loss, by what we are given in the next moment.

Time does heal. The healing comes in watching the fire of time consume without fighting to save anything from the flame—allowing the next and the next and the next thing to change. The loss is necessary, required by the choice to live in a burning world, a place where we are destined to hold desperately, love, and let go at the same time.

We live, Jordan says, in a burning world.
Everything will be lost.

What is it like for you to experience loss and
change all around you? To love people
and things and know that time will
alter and take them?

What has the impermanence of
things taught you?
....

～ Time and Reality ～

*Time is a lake, and we drop each choice, each change
into it. Each choice, each change makes ripples,
all crisscrossing and intersecting until every molecule
of the water has been touched and affected. Each
event displaces something else that could have happened,
in the same way a thrown stone displaces water
as it breaks the surface of the lake.*

Jordan suggests that each choice we make displaces another choice, something else we could have done. The ripple effect of each choice touches everything during and after that moment.

How do the ripples reach you? How do you feel the timeline of all that was possible narrows to your one choice and outcome?

How do the ripples of others' choices reach you?

. . . .

∼ Time in the Physical and Spirit Worlds ∼

Time exists both here on Earth and in the spirit world. In both places time's sole function is to mark change. Here, time marks physical changes—the moving hands of a clock, a car driving from Boston to New York, an exploding supernova. In the spirit world, time marks changes in consciousness. It measures the growth of awareness, the before and after of a thought, an image, or a creation. In the spirit world, time also measures the growth of one's personal consciousness, the before and after of each new awareness we form.

Time marks change, both on Earth and in the spirit world. Learning is a form of change—and there is always a time *before* and *after* each thing we learn. Our consciousness changes with every lesson in life.

What changes has time brought you that taught you the most?

What are some of the things you've learned that had a *before* and *after* quality?

· ·

～ Observing History ～

While time in the spirit and physical worlds does the same thing, spirit world time is both outside of, and independent from, physical world time. From the spirit world we can watch the physical universe at any time in its history. We can watch the big bang, the dinosaur age, the breaking up of Pangea to form continents. All of history can be observed. On the timeline of spirit we continue to grow and evolve with everything learned, each lifetime lived.

All of history from every planet, every decision made and every choice not taken, is recorded in the Akashic record. We study it—the most important textbook of the afterlife— to learn the outcome of every soul's decisions: what goes well and what doesn't, what strengthens love and what disconnects us.

If you could watch any event in history unfold,
what would you choose to watch? Why?

How do you feel about watching your
previous lives unfold?

Is there anything you wouldn't want to relive?
What might you learn from that recognition?
....

7

Discerning Reality

Illusion vs. Meaning

IS WHAT WE EXPERIENCE as real—our relationships and the world around us—a dream, an illusion? Or do the laws of physics that we all experience, as well as the emotional experiences we have in common, prove that not to be true? In either case, what is the reason for all that we feel and experience? What gives our struggles here meaning?

There are philosophers and mystics who say we live in the midst of a dream, that nothing is real. They suggest no reason for the illusion we call the world, except that it is some aberration of consciousness or a backdrop for diverting stories living in the mind of God. In this scenario, perhaps even the dreamer, the protagonist of the illusion, isn't real—just some dissociated part of one, nondual consciousness (All or God). Others claim that there isn't one shared dream, but many. That each dreamer has a separate world, perhaps interfacing here and there with others, yet always private and unrelated by cause and effect to any other dream.

So we struggle to know if anything is real. And if what we experience is unreal—even ourselves—then nothing faced in this life matters. It has no meaning.

On the other hand, if this were not a shared reality, with predictable laws and outcomes, we couldn't learn from each other. We couldn't observe and communicate common experiences. For example, without a shared experience of the physics of friction and flight, one pitcher couldn't learn from another about release point, spin, movement, resistance, and all the other mechanics of throwing a ball. Without a shared understanding of the emotion of loss, no soul could have compassion for another's painful struggles with impermanence. Without a shared understanding of desire, no one could experience the other's hunger, or recognize the bitter taste of despair when all that was sought slips forever out of reach. We share this reality for a reason, a purpose that unites every soul who comes here. The purpose is to learn, and this gives meaning to our life.

∼ The Material World Teaches ∼

The idea that the material world is an illusion—either individually or collectively—misses the point of why the physical universe exists. The physical universe does have a purpose, a reason to be. It is not an accident of mind; it's our classroom.

We know each consciousness evolves and grows in relationship to the physical world through experience. Every struggle we face on Earth teaches us something. We grow more aware and wise. We see more clearly the consequences of our acts and how the ripples of cause and effect touch everything and everyone in our lives.

All consciousness seeks to learn—from the individual soul to All. The intention to learn is the progenitor of everything that we see and think. Reality, the world, was created for us to love and learn in.

Jordan suggests that the physical world is real,
not an illusion, and that it exists to teach us—
both individual souls and God—
important lessons.

If you were designing the world, what lessons
would you want it to teach?

What struggles are necessary to our individual
growth and evolution?

What struggles do you think are needed
for All to grow and evolve?
....

~ Finding Meaning ~

We have all been dropped here on a moonless night.
Reaching blindly, we learn by the feel of things with each
dark thing we touch. We stumble in the dark and see what
happens with each unseen step. And then the moon comes
out and in that dim light we see a little of what was hidden.
We see the trees but not the forest, a path but not the
destination, the movement of leaves and branches but not
the wind, the Earth beneath our feet but not what holds us.
We wait. Every moment continues to teach. Some truth of
everything we see or touch arrives without asking for it.

This is our purpose, our meaning—to know ourselves and
distill some truth from our experience. This is what we come
to Earth to do. The shared reality of the material universe
was created for this reason. Rather than be meaningless and
absurd, every object—including ourselves—was made real
not only so we can grow and evolve but so All could grow
and evolve. A stable physical world—with laws and love and
often painful outcomes—is the plane on
which all consciousness expands.

How have you discovered or located
meaning in your life?

What truths have you distilled from
your experience?

Was there a time, a "moonless night," when
you couldn't yet find your meaning?

How did that time feel?
. . . .

∼ Everything Changes, but Something Remains ∼

Matter, forms, "things" evolve and devolve, growing in complexity—and then they erode. Think of layer upon layer of sedimentary rock, gathering mud and minerals, pressing together, hardening. And then glaciers scrape the rock, rivers cut through it, and wind and rain wear it away, only to have the broken rock buried in a lava flow. The impermanence of matter, of reality, teaches us.

Yet consciousness never erodes. Our soul, unlike our brain, never forgets. We take with us every lesson. Everything we love teaches us, every moment of pain and every struggle teaches us. Each new thing we learn is sewn forever into our soul consciousness.

What are the lessons you brought into
to this life?

What are the lessons, so far, you will
take with you from this life?
. . . .

.

How to Channel

CHANNELING FOR EVERYONE

Channeling is not the exclusive province of mystics, prophets, seers, or mediums. It requires no special gifts of clairaudience, no access to spiritual visions, no ordination into a mystery school or any form of priesthood. Channeling is like prayer—anyone can do it. *You* can do it if you care to follow the simple steps of the process and begin a two-way communication to entities in spirit. They are a thought away. The mere *intention* to communicate opens the channel.*

STEPS TO THE CHANNELING PROCESS

1. Select a place to channel that supports feeling safe and grounded. It could be a solid-feeling desk or

---

*The following process first appeared in my book *The Luminous Landscape of the Afterlife*, pages 105–10.

table or in a chair that you associate with comfort and calm.

2. Decide on a spiritual address to send your questions and messages. Is there a particular loved soul, now in the afterlife, with whom you want to communicate? Do you want to send questions to your spirit guide, the one who supports and watches over you? Another choice would be to send questions and messages to the part of your own soul that always remains in spirit—to communicate with your higher self, your own soul knowledge. You might also choose to communicate with the Divine, All, God. Before attempting to channel, be clear which entity you are seeking to reach.

3. Select a talisman—an object that represents your connection to the entity you'll channel. If it's someone you loved on Earth who is now in spirit, you might use an object that belonged to them or that they gave to you. Otherwise choose a talisman that symbolizes your spirit guide, higher self, or God— whichever you plan to channel. Mandalas, sacred stones, crystals, Buddhist or Celtic knots, and other symbols of spirit are often used.

4. Use an object—candles work well—for eye fixation. If you choose a candle flame for your focus, find a base that's pleasing in a color you associate with peace, nature, or spiritual connection. Always

use the same base—the accouterments of ritual are important.

5. Take a breath, and as you slowly exhale, feel the *intention* to make contact, to open the channel.

6. Begin a mindful breath meditation. This meditation creates a mild altered state—a doorway to the other side

   • Focus awareness on the diaphragm—the genesis and center of your breath. Breathe in and out slowly.

   • On your first out-breath, count *one*; with your second out-breath count *two*, and so on until you reach *ten*. Repeat for one or two more cycles of ten breaths, or until you feel significantly relaxed and receptive.

   • When a thought arises, notice but don't dwell on the thought. Return your attention as soon as possible to your breath. Thoughts will always show up during meditation; this is normal and should never be judged as some sort of failure. Your only task is to return awareness to your breath each time you notice a thought.

   • Keep watching the candle flame throughout your meditation.

7. Use a light divination to expand openness and receptivity by imagining an orb of light about

six inches above your head. It is a reflection of the candle flame before you. Now visualize the orb expanding upward until it is a shaft of yellow light—the color of the sun. This light above you is the channel, the connecting place between you and those in the spirit world (your loved ones, spirit guides, your own soul in spirit, or God). The channel is now open. And your mere *intention* to connect keeps it so.

8. Keep a record of every channeled conversation. You will find it important to review this over time, as there will be much wisdom in your journal. In a special notebook that you keep only for channeling, physically write your first question. Maintain openness to whatever you receive in response to your question.

9. Watch the words form on the page. The answer will show up in a variety of ways. Usually, in the beginning, the communication is halting. A word or two will come. Just write them down without judging or trying to understand what they mean. Listen to the voice in your mind. After the first word or two, wait. Stay open to receive the next phrase or the rest of the sentence—and write that down too. Wait again—there may be more.

Note that the communications you receive can take other forms, especially as you get more practiced at channeling. These alternate forms can include:

- The download. These are complete and complex ideas that *you* have to find words to describe. The communication comes only as a picture, a diagram, or a concept.

- The rush. This is a series of words and sentences that come rapid fire—often faster than you can write.

- The telescoped answer. Often this can be one or two potent words, such as "all love . . . stay . . . always . . . with you," and so on.

10. When there is a period of silence and the communication has apparently stopped, write down your next question. Continue this process until needing to rest or sensing that you've done enough. Because channeled answers, particularly at the beginning, are often so brief, you might consider asking simple yes-or-no questions at the start.

11. Accept the inevitable doubts and judgments that arise. There is no way to have certainty that the voice in your mind is the soul or guide or divinity you've addressed. And you will periodically have doubt or fear that channeling is a form of self-deception. Keep channeling in the face of these thoughts—everyone has them. If you persevere, you will acquire—over time—a written body of love, wisdom, and deep knowledge.

It will move you; it will support you; it will guide you.

Things You Can Ask via Channeling

- Try simple yes-or-no questions at the beginning—"Are you happy?" for example.

- Ask questions, if you're interested, about the soul's transition.

- Ask for advice or support.

- Ask about the nature of the afterlife.

- Ask about your life purpose, your direction.

- Ask for wisdom to make good choices.

- Ask how best to love and how to act on love in daily life.

- Ask for or offer forgiveness.

- Ask for help facing difficult things, painful emotions, or destructive desires and impulses.

Things Not to Ask for While Channeling

- The future is off limits in channeling. Entities from the spirit world are not allowed to reveal the future because such knowledge prevents you from learning and making decisions of free will.

- Entities from the other side, with rare exceptions, cannot fix things. What they *can* do is support you to make the wisest choices as you face challenging situations. Don't ask for intercessions, for the course of events to change, or for help unraveling problems.

- Medical intercessions are beyond the allowed capabilities of discarnate souls or guides. Asking for medical cures or changes in prognosis can result in channel blockage. The souls on the other side can't give this to you, and your determination to get help may prevent you from hearing their response.

- Entities from spirit can't change the behavior of others. They can't get a child to stop self-destructive patterns, make a landlord say "yes" if you need a place to live, push a potential employer to give you a job, or help your team win the Super Bowl.

- Pain relief isn't a role for discarnate souls or spirit guides. Don't ask entities on the other side to take away suffering or protect you from painful experiences on Earth. They will help you face pain, but not avoid it.

BOOKS OF RELATED INTEREST

The Luminous Landscape of the Afterlife
Jordan's Message to the Living on What to Expect after Death
by Matthew McKay, Ph.D.

Love in the Time of Impermanence
by Matthew McKay, Ph.D.

7 Reasons to Believe in the Afterlife
A Doctor Reviews the Case for Consciousness after Death
by Jean Jacques Charbonier, M.D.

The Persistence of the Soul
Mediums, Spirit Visitations, and Afterlife Communication
by Mark Ireland

Healing Wisdom from the Afterlife
How to Communicate with the Spirit World
by Alexandra Leclere

Heal Your Ancestral Roots
Release the Family Patterns That Hold You Back
by Anuradha Dayal-Gulati, Ph.D.

Ancestral Medicine
Rituals for Personal and Family Healing
by Daniel Foor, Ph.D.

A New Science of the Afterlife
Space, Time, and the Consciousness Code
by Daniel Drasin

INNER TRADITIONS • BEAR & COMPANY
P.O. Box 388
Rochester, VT 05767
1-800-246-8648
www.InnerTraditions.com

Or contact your local bookseller